WORDS at play

by JOHN H. KOESTER

Words at Play

Published by JH Koester, LLC

1404 E Graham Ranch Trail

Payson, AZ 85541

www.JohnKoesterBooks.com

LCCN
2020919318

ISBN
978-1-7358784-0-9

Cover Art Desgin, Illustration, Editing, & Layout by StarwhaleBooks.com

CAN POETRY WIN A GIRL'S HEART? IT SURE CAN!

From the time we met, John would recite poetry to me. Over the years we've been married, I've never grown tired of hearing him share his poems with others, whether they're total strangers, family, or friends. I am so excited to see his writings finally published for the world to enjoy. These poems will make you ponder. These poems will make you smile. They may even make you cry. Enjoy the words and illustrations as they play on the pages together.

~ **Rachel Koester**

NOTE FROM THE AUTHOR

All my life I have dreamed up stories to explain to myself and to others how and why I feel the way I do. Poetry is storytelling and, in many cases, the message surprises the reader and sometimes the author and storyteller. I am an inventor. I invent solutions to existing problems in my industry. Poetry is very similar. Poems are a solution, or an explanation, to scenarios that exist in one's life.

ABOUT THE BOOK COVER

It was a dream that helped me truly understand myself. I am my own worst enemy.

WORDS
at play

by JOHN H. KOESTER

WORDS AT PLAY

I need to write a poem today
Disguised to sound like words at play,
But in its rhyme, some worth to say
To help mankind along its way.
I need to write a poem today.

ASK FOR MUCH

Take a step forward
On an unknown path,
Enter the future with questions to ask.
Have what you wished for
Hold life in your grasp.
Write your own play
Choose your own cast
And have a cool pillow
To hear your last gasp.

EVERY DAY

Every day, I'm not the same again.
Changed from without
Or changed from within.
Is it the committing,
Or just the knowing of sin?
But every day, I'm not the same again.

CHOIR BOY

Once, I was a choir boy,
And then I got defrocked.
The scene, it was the crying room,
But crying there was not.
The happy sounds of moans and groans
Had given us away.
Once, I was a choir boy,
But not as of today.

THE POOL HALL

Corley and Franny and the hard work put in.
The condoms I bought, to cover my sin.
The clouds of blue smoke that hung end to end.
The smell of cheap beer that had been processed through men.
Not the first to experience or to ignore,
The perils of entering
The pool hall's back door.

The Pool Hall smelled. Pool halls are supposed to smell. The Pool Hall had a bad reputation. Pool halls, if they are good, do. Pool halls need a back door and it should always lead to a dark alley. This one did. The patrons of any pool hall progress from sneaking in the back door to sitting in the front booths or standing at the bar, and then proudly leaving through the front door. Like all things in life, once you cross certain thresholds, you are never the same again.

"BIG HAT"

You can't be a cowboy
Without a
"Big Hat."
Tall boots, loud spurs,
And heels that aren't flat.
Wide belt, big buckle,
With your name on the back.
But you can't be a cowboy,
Without a
"Big Hat."

PAINS

Pains are my friends.
I have quite a few.
We sit in the darkness,
Enjoying the view.

WANT TO BE COWBOY "STRAIGHT UP"

If you have never named a horse,
You have never owned one.
If you have never been with cowgirls,
You've never had no fun.
Now, wearing boots and cowboy hats may
Make you feel that way,
But, until you've been with cowgirls,
There just isn't much to say.

HOT SUMMER'S EVE

All the way in my blue Chevrolet.
Down the road from that pile of hay
On the eve of a hot summer's day
Naked as jaybirds in every way
Happy in heart, I'm glad to say
Cross the eyes of those that just prayed
All the way in my blue Chevrolet.

PLUMBER'S SONG

It's more than just a plumber's song,
It's a pipe that clogged,
It's a turd gone wrong.
It's a shit or piss
That won't go down.
It's a housewife
With a surly frown.
Then he arrives,
This knight in blue,
A wrench, a bit, a pipe to screw.
And when he's through,
All smiles abound,
Because everyone knows
The shit went down.

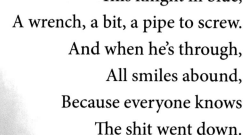

WISHES

I wished
Things were different.
There are things
I wished I could change.
But maybe
That is what wishes are for,
They help
To ease the pain.

THESE EYES

I see myself a cowboy.
I ride my horse so fast.
Up and down the dusty roads
And through the prairie grass.
Up the sides of mountains,
Almost to the sky.
I see myself a cowboy…
But only through these eyes.

PERCEIVED VALUE

If you love your dogs
And they love you back,
You're richer by far
Than gold coins in a stack.
Rubies and pearls,
To fill a large sack.
If you love your dogs
And they love you back.

DANCING FARMER

There's a little town
Beside the road,
That no one knows
And no one goes.
And Sunday aft,
They play some pros
And no one listens…
But people come from miles around
To see the dancing farmer.

Often poets write poems that have meaning for themselves alone or for a select group. This is the case for the Dancing Farmer. There will be a few who read this poem and know everything about the place and all the characters in it. For others, I am sorry, but you just had to have been there.

RATIONAL ACT

I just finished justifying a rational act,
That I committed a little while back.
I knew in the moment
It was the right thing to do,
It just took some time
To think it all through.
And why should I suffer
The pain caused by shame?
When I've been blessed
With this wonderful brain.

KNOWING

I thought I was a man
That could read nature's signs.
Just short of a man
That could read people's minds.
And now, that I know,
I don't even know mine.

THE GIFT

On legs that never tire,
On walks that never end.
That is what we wish for
And death grants that wish, my friend.
With a gift of loving memories
Of a strong and loyal friend.
On legs that never tire,
On walks that never end.

BUTCHER'S DOG

I wished I was a butcher's dog.
I'd be fatter than a corn-fed hog
With a T-bone for breakfast every day
And pot roast for supper on a steel tray.
Now wishful thinking, this is for sure
Cause I'm just a common street-bred cur.
But wishes are wishes
And dreams do come true.
So, while you're at it,
Bring a pork chop or two.

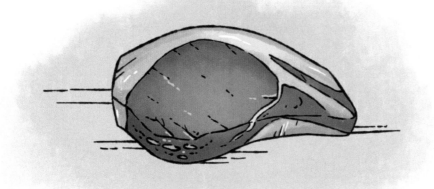

THE NEW TRUE

If it was not true,
If it was not true,
And everyone knows
It was not true,
Then how can it be true,
When known by so few…
"The world is round."

DOG POOP

Picking up dog poop,
Picking up dog poop.
Short fat and round ones,
Big dark and brown ones.
Picking up dog poop.

FIND 'EM WITH OUR FEET

Smelly little piles
From stinky little seats.
We walk around and
Find 'em with our feet.
Find 'em with our feet,
Smelly little piles
From stinky little seats.

SPARROW

I never heard the sparrow's song
Until I neared the end.
I was racing down life's highway
With energy to spend.
I should have stopped and listened
And made his song my friend.
Is it better that I hear it now
When I never heard it then?

FACTS

I wished I knew,
I wished I knew,
The things that make it false or true.
Who heard by eyes
And seen by ears,
Of different sorts.

HARD TO GET TO HEAVEN

It's hard to get to heaven,
If you've been liven while you're living.
Now, I've been just enjoying
All the things God has given.
Now, they come to tell me,
I've been just a sinnen.
Hard to get to heaven,
When you've been liven while you're living.

MISSED OPPORTUNITY

There was a time when I thought
My vote did count.
But now I wonder,
As I look about.
History will record
This time and this date,
When good men and women
Fail to participate.

HORSES DYING FOR A CHANGE

They had to know as man, they were led to change.
They knew his hand and now they knew his pain,
And it was theirs.
A week, a month, or more had come to pass
With no harness and long days of sweet grass
A peaceful rest, as in the past
Between the planting of the fields
And reaping of hay grass.
Too long, too long,
And time was wrong.

ONE KNOWS

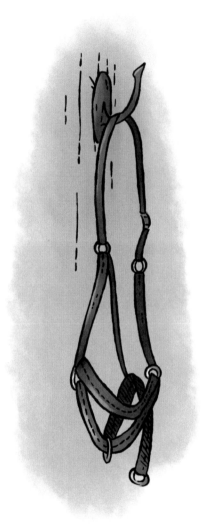

It's just old sweat-stained leather
That hangs on the wall,
And some broken boards
From an empty stall.
To most that walk by
These things mean nothing at all.
Except, for the man that knew
The horses that lived there,
And killed them.

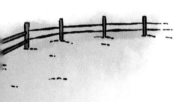

During the late 40s and early 50s there was a transition in the agricultural industry from horse-drawn to gasoline-powered farm equipment. The teams of horses that worked alongside the farmers became obsolete. This was the case on the farm I grew up on. The economy was such that there were numerous teams of horses that could not be supported. They were sold to mink ranchers for meat for feed. Everyone has heard the phrase, "Change is hard." This change was sending your horses, your workmates, to their death. My father never forgave himself for killing his horses. They were his friends.

APPLAUSE

The loud applause will end,
And with it that feeling, my friend.
Don't sit and face silence
Till it happens again.
That loud applause, my friend.

GETTING OLD

Getting old, is getting old.

Gone are the days of young and bold.

Near the days

When this gig folds…

Getting old, is getting old.

TATTOOS

My body is a billboard,
It has a story to tell.
My life has been shitty,
Close to pure hell.
With the name of my girlfriend,
That she helped me to spell.
My body is a billboard,
It has a story to tell.

EXPLAINING DIVORCE

You think you saw a ghost last night.
Well, maybe it was me.
The one you lived with most your life
And didn't really see.
The one you shared your days with
And all those lonely nights.
You think you saw a ghost last night.
Well, how would you know
If it was me?

BUTTERFLIES

Not just the one
That owns your eye.
It's true of all butterflies.
The wind is changed
When they fly,
And it's not for us to know
How much or why.

TO THE VICTOR GOES HISTORY

Who's wrong,
Who's right?
Who's wrong,
Who's right?
Of those, that struggle
With all their might,
To survive the dark,
To see dawn's light,
To tell the tale.
Who's wrong,
Who's right?

JUNE BUGS

June
With no June bugs,
But what do they know?
When May was so cold
And all of that snow.
And where's the corn,
And where's the beans?
And why this strange weather,
And what does it mean?
But then again,
What do June bugs know?

CORN

Not everyone knows corn can talk,
With lips of green leaves on every stalk.
With a choir of voices, it can sing,
In early Summer and late Spring.

And corn can see and that's no lie,
With fireflies for its eyes,
And dewdrops for its tears at dawn.
And everyone knows corn can hear,
With rows and rows of those great ears.

O' OUTHOUSE

O' outhouse,
O' outhouse,
Do you remember me?
The rosy-cheeked man
You met last week.
Chili dinner,
Budweiser pee.

A SIN

It's a sin
When a man can't fart.
The place
Where all true laughter starts.
And why
Us, sophisticated folk,
Think a squeaky fart
Is still a joke.

SO FEW

So few,
So few,
Survive the loves they knew…
Or want to,
But we do.

RISKING A HEART ATTACK

The only reason to shovel snow
Is to clear a path so you can go
Someplace far or someplace near
Where slipping and falling is never a fear.

HIP PITY HOP

Little bunny goes hip pity hop.
Got the rabbit habit
And he can't stop.

IT'S A THRILL

There once was a man named Al Gore
And when approached by a whore, he said,
"It's a thrill, but you're looking for Bill,
And he lives in that Whitehouse next door."

SOCIALLY ACCEPTABLE

The hard-working hooker
Nearly wore out her bum,
But the butcher made more
With the weight of this thumb.

DISCONNECTED

If things could be disconnected,
They just wouldn't be the same.
Without the wind to bring the clouds,
There'd probably be no rain.

THE SPOON

Like the spoon that stirs the stew,
To know all the flavors in it,
But never to be nourished
By a bowl of it.

STRONG

The proof that you are really strong
Is your ability to admit you could be wrong.

HAMMER THE EARTH INTO SWORDS

I stand with sword in hand
And wonder at this beauty's strand,
And then with movement swift,
The sword is taken from my fist,
And cuts away my neighbor's life.
Then at my feet
The broken sword laid down.
I think of rock, which made the sword
And wonder,
Is man better than this?

My neighbor to my other side cries out,
"You think of rock
When my neighbor's life is gone.
How price you life?"
And my reply…
 "With currency of sunny days
A million fold."
Again, he screams,
"You think of rock."
And my reply…
"What are sunny days
Without a rock to shine upon?"

This poem was my first. It was 1970 and the Vietnam war was going on. The constant of human nature is war. It will be the end of us all and, worse than that, it will be the end of our planet if we do not change.

DOORWAY

There is never a door
Without a doorway,
And with it the question,
To go or to stay.

KISSES

I love to give her kisses,
And when I can't
My heart, it misses
All her sweet
And loving kisses.

LISTEN AND HEAR

If you have heard the wind blow,
A babbling creek flow,
Or the silence of falling snow…
You have heard a poem.

TRACKS

Until the first snow does fall,
You know not who your neighbors are.
Tracks.

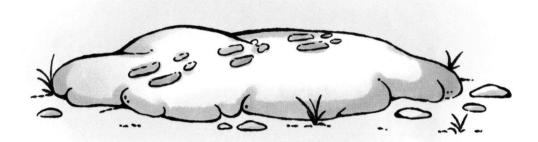

WHAT WE SEE

Looking at the moon
Looking at me.
Always the question,
What do we see?

LOVE AFFAIR

The pain of
A sad love affair
Is second to none,
Except for
The life lived
That has never known one.

PERFECT

If I look in the mirror
And it's perfect I see,
I know for darn sure,
It's not really me.

PAPERWORK

You white-throated ceramic devil,
First cousin to the bidet.
I stand before you,
I kneel before you,
I bend over for you,
I give you my indulgence.
Wash them away.
P.S.
I'll do the paperwork.

MEMORY

There is a problem with the ability
To never forget…
You can live in the past.

THE LESSON LEARNED

You can learn a lesson from books.
You can learn a lesson from life.
You can learn a lesson from good times.
You can learn a lesson from strife.
But who could ever guess,
How could anyone know,
You can even learn a lesson,
From sharing a lowly potato.

You do not share with others
In need to help them.
You share with others
In need to help yourself.

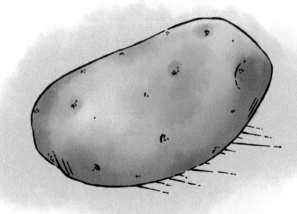

My first three years of school were in a one room schoolhouse on the northwest corner of our farm. In the cold months of the school year, the building was heated by an oil burning furnace that sat in one corner. We would bring potatoes to school, all twelve of us, and bake them on top of the furnace. When someone forgot their potato or their potato was bad, everyone would take part of their potato and share it with the person with no potato. There was an unannounced contest of who would give the biggest piece of their potato. I never forgot to bring a potato or had a bad one, so I learned how to share, but not how to be gracious. Some things are not natural, they must be learned.

UNKNOWN

Take an unknown path
And you may trip
And you may fall,
But would it be worse
Than not knowing or
Going at all?

Made in the USA
Middletown, DE
02 November 2020